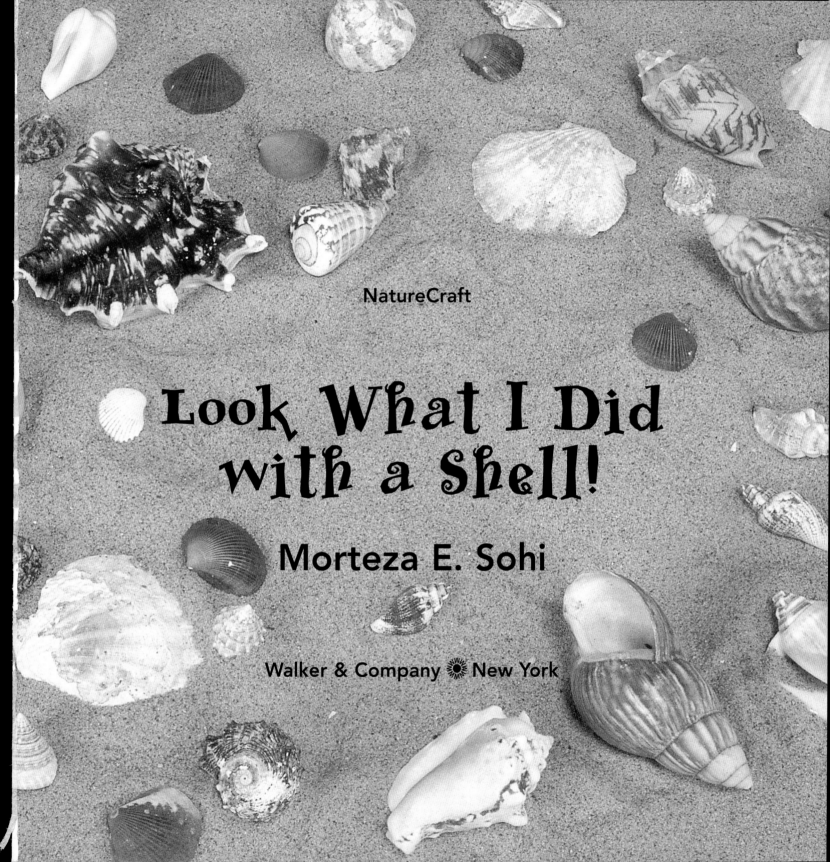

NatureCraft

Look What I Did with a Shell!

Morteza E. Sohi

Walker & Company ✹ New York

Special thanks to Paula M. Mikkelsen, Ph.D., of the American Museum of Natural History, for helping to identify the shells in the Field Guide.

First published in the United States of America in 2000 by Walker Publishing Company, Inc.

Published simultaneously in Canada by Fitzhenry and Whiteside, Markham, Ontario L3R 4T8

Library of Congress Cataloging-in-Publication Data available upon request

Book design by Sophie Ye Chin

Printed in Hong Kong
2 4 6 8 10 9 7 5 3 1

Many people believe that they can hear the ocean when they listen to shells. No wonder! Wherever there is an ocean, there are shells.

There are over 60,000 different seashells worldwide. Shells can curve gracefully or twist like corkscrews. They can be brown, gray, white, pink, purple, or blue. These jewels of the beach can be used to create animal sculptures and shell gardens, or to decorate jewelry boxes, picture frames, and other gifts.

COLLECTING SHELLS

Shells are fun to collect and keep. You can find them along sandy beaches, in shallow coastal waters, or on rocky shores. Many of the most colorful shells are found in deep water and by coral reefs. They have to be collected by deep-sea divers. You can't collect these by yourself, but you can buy them at craft shops.

Do's and Don'ts

- Do collect shells at low tide. Make sure you can reach safety if the tide starts to come in.
- Don't forget that beaches can be dangerous places.
- Do make sure somebody knows where you are, and always go with a friend.
- Don't do any damage to the environment.
- Do ask permission before crossing private property to reach a beach.
- Don't take more shells than you need.
- Do have fun!

Shell Collecting Equipment

- Bags or pails to put the shells in.
- A magnifying glass to examine the shells.
- Shallow containers lined with cotton for delicate shells.
- Garden tools—a small spade, shovel, or garden fork to dig out bivalves.
- A small colander to strain out very small shells from sand and mud and for cleaning sand off the shells.

You will need the right clothing and equipment when you go shell hunting. The sun at the beach can be very strong, and you can easily become sunburned. Use sunscreen and wear a T-shirt and sun hat. On rocky beaches the rocks can cut your feet, so always have waterproof shoes with you.

TRAINING YOUR ARTIST'S EYE

When you paint a picture or make a collage, you choose different colors and shapes to create the look you want.

Contrast

Contrast is an important technique to use. Do you see how the dark shells on the wings, eyes, ears, and beak of the owl stand out against the light cream-colored shell used for its body? The brown and black and the cream are contrasting colors because they are so different from one another.

Art Notes

Have you thought about where you are going to sit when you work on your shell animals? It may not seem important, but it is. All artists like to have a space in which they can create. Here are some tips for setting up a workspace that will help you be a better artist. You will need:

• A large, flat surface to work on and a comfortable seat.
• A place to leave your drying sculptures for up to 48 hours where they will not be disturbed.
• QUIET.

Make sure that your work surface is completely clean before you begin work and always clean up after you have completed your project.

Shape

Shells come in many different shapes. When you see these different shapes, think about how you can use them to make your shell animals.

CORKSCREW

OVAL

WRAPAROUND

FAN

ROUND

Oval-shaped cowrie shells are great for basic body parts. The dog has a cowrie shell head. The rabbit's body is also made from this very useful shell.

Moon and nutmeg shells are round like wheels and make good snail shells.

Size

You also have to think about size. The large shells used to make this polar bear are perfect for an animal's body and head.

Smaller shells can be used for the animal's facial features—like the nose and eyes on this mouse. You can also use smaller shells for ears, paws, and tails.

Art Notes

Have you decided what kind of shell animal you would like to make? Try drawing a sketch of the animal before you begin work. Pay attention to how big the head is. Do you have the right shells put aside for ears or paws?

Some artists like to have all their materials arranged in order before they begin a project. Try organizing your shells in groups according to size, shape, color, and texture. This will help you find a particular shell easily when you need it.

Color

When you paint or draw, you usually use lots of colors to make your art project bright and colorful. Shells can be colorful too. Shells from warmer waters are usually more vivid than shells from colder seas. Many shells are decorated with pretty patterns.

You can make this cat with tortoise-patterned shells. The pink inlay in the smaller shell looks like the inside of a cat's ears. Use dried seaweed to make whiskers.

Art Notes

Many artists need reference materials. This means that they need something to look at while they are working. Some artists take photographs of people in different poses and draw from the photos. This helps them capture the image they want.

You might find it useful to have reference materials for your shell animals. Look at magazines, toy catalogs, greeting cards, and picture books. The picture doesn't have to be of a real animal—it could be of a cartoon or a toy. Maybe there is an animal character that you want to try to make, like Babar or Curious George. Never tear anything out of a magazine without getting permission. Your librarian can show you how to copy a picture from a book.

Texture

Run your fingers over a few shells. Some feel silky smooth and others are bumpy with knobby ridges and ribs.

You can use these textures to create more lifelike animal features. The ribbing on fan-shaped shells will help you make feathered wings for this bird.

Knobby, spiral-shaped shells make great legs for goats, sheep, or even dogs. Spiny cords and ribs can resemble wooly coats for furry creatures or even hard, scaly skin for reptiles and amphibians.

ASSEMBLING THE ANIMALS

Preparing the Shells

When you get home from the beach, clean the shells by soaking them in a bowl of warm water. Handle the shells gently so that you don't break them or cut yourself on sharp edges. You can brush off the sand or mud with a small nailbrush or a toothbrush. Dry the shells carefully with paper towels. Make sure you remove all the excess water.

Art Notes

Here are the materials you will need in addition to your shells:

- Plastic sheeting or newspaper to cover your work surface to protect it from glue.
- Nontoxic tacky glue—available from craft shops. Elmer's blue tacky glue is a good choice. Ask a clerk to recommend nontoxic tacky glue. Double-check the label. Don't use rubber cement or model glue for this project.
- Cotton swabs. Use them to clean up extra glue. They are also good for pushing tiny shells into place.
- Modeling clay. Form a mold around the shell sculpture to keep it tightly bound while the glue dries.
- Glue brush.

Putting It All Together

Lay the shells on your work surface and arrange different shells until you find the best combination. For example, here is how to put a ram together. Choose two big, round shells (like clamshells) for the body and an oval-shaped shell for the head. Carefully glue on two small curly shaped shells for horns and two small round shells for eyes—or plastic eyes if necessary. Don't forget to add two small oval or triangular-shaped shells as ears.

Don't glue more than two shells together at a time, and let them dry before adding more. Some shell shapes will require more glue than others to get them to really stick together. You can use modeling clay to help bind the shells for additional support. Let the animal dry for at least one day. Some animals will need two days to dry.

Shells that are slim and pointed should have glue applied to their openings and be supported by surrounding shells. One shell will balance on top of another only if their two surfaces fit together.

Layering Techniques

You can layer shells of different colors, shapes, and sizes to make elephant trunks, tails, nesting birds, plants, and vegetation. Layering shells will help you build height and add depth to your shell sculptures.

Look at the next page to see how you can layer shells of different sizes and colors to form a realistic looking elephant trunk. Find 10 to 13 shells of similar shape in different sizes. Glue the shells together, one at a time, beginning with the largest shell and ending with the smallest, to create a trunklike shape.

After you've gotten more experience, you can use layering to create animal families like the two birds nesting on a clump of mushrooms below.

MAKE A SCENE

Don't limit yourself to designing only one animal at a time. You can create a scene using a large shell as a base and glue small shell sculptures on top of it. You can also create backdrops for bigger scenes.

Polar Scene

Imagine a snow scene using cotton balls or gauze, silver foil for icy water, and a painted backdrop of bright white and silver-blue. You've created the perfect habitat for penguin and polar bear shell sculptures.

Forest Scene

Try creating a forest scene with bird sculptures, rabbits, squirrels, toadstools, an owl, and some mice. Use a shallow tray or lid and cover the base with dirt, mulch, or soft material. Make trees and bushes out of rolled-up cardboard or modeling clay and pipe cleaners. Paint a circular area to look like a pond and decorate it with lily pads and small stones.

GREAT GIFTS YOU CAN MAKE

Shells make excellent decorations. Some of the large tropical shells are ornaments on their own, but many small shells can be used to decorate other objects.

Decorative Objects

The best way to attach the shells to the object you wish to decorate—a box, vase, or bottle—is to put a layer of modeling clay over the object. Press the shells into the clay to make a pattern, using shells of different sizes and colors. After the clay dries, you can coat the object with varnish to protect it and give it a glossy finish.

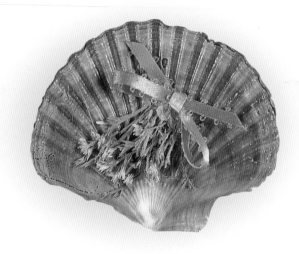

Decorative Frames

You can use shells to decorate an old picture frame or a mirror. Apply an even coat of modeling clay to the frame and then stick the shells onto the sticky surface. Wait for the surface to dry and paint it if you choose.

Shell Garden

Fill a shoebox lid with a shallow layer of sand. Use a fork to create swirls or geometric patterns in the sand. Decorate the sand with interesting shells.

THE LIFE CYCLE OF A MOLLUSK

The shells you've collected were once the homes of sea animals called mollusks. Different species of mollusks reproduce in different ways. Some mollusks leave their eggs to float freely in the water. Others hide them in the sand in a living sponge, or even in their own bodies. Some species of mollusks have males and females, just like humans. In other mollusks, the same animal is both male and female.

As the mollusk grows, its shell grows with it. When it is fully formed, it will be ready to produce eggs. Mollusks lay masses of eggs, because only a few will survive. An egg hatches into a larva and eventually the larva begins to grow a shell. The larva swims until it finds a rock or other place to settle and grow.

After a sea animal dies, its shell is often turned into a home by other animals and plants. Many shells have two halves that hinge together. After the owner dies, the two halves may become separated.

Mollusk Glossary

Although there are six kinds of mollusks, only four are of interest to shell collectors. Cephalopods are carnivorous mollusks without shells. And monoplacophoras are very rare and live only in the deepest water.

GASTROPODS have a single shell. They include snails, periwinkles, whelks, and conches. Most have a coiled shell, although some have a cap-shaped shell.

BIVALVES have two shells, or valves, hinged together. They include clams, oysters, and scallops.

SCAPHOPODS are known as tusk or tooth shells. They are open at both ends. They bury themselves in the sand with only the narrow end sticking out to suck in water.

POLYPLACOPHORAS are known as chitons or "coat of mail" shells. They have eight shell plates, bound together at the sides by a leatherlike belt.

FIELD GUIDE

Here are the common names, types, and family names, as well as general information about the size, diet, and habitat of many of the shells used to make the animals in this book. When creating your own shell animals, you may use whatever shells are available to you.

Ceriths (Common Vertegas) Gastropod; Family: Cerithiidae

There are 300 species of ceriths inhabiting sandy places around coral reefs; they are widely distributed in shallow, tropical seas. Ceriths are 1 to 5 inches long, and are generally defined with many whorls and distinct sculpturing and patterns. All are vegetarians.

Cockles (Giant Heart Cockle) Bivalve; Family: Cardiidae

Cockles are a large group of colorful species with an array of shapes showing all degrees of sculpturing. They are oval to almost circular, 1½ to 6 inches long. Occasionally, they are squarish or flattened and triangular. Cockles inhabit locations worldwide in both shallow and deep water where they feed on plankton and other microorganisms that they filter from the water. Cockles are active animals that can jump several inches by means of a long, powerful foot.

Cones (Purple Cone) Gastropod; Family: Conidae

There are 400 species of cones living in warm waters around the world; they are from ¾ to 12 inches long. Cones are carnivorous, feeding on other mollusks, worms, and small fish. They stun their prey before consuming it by injecting it with venom.

Cowrie Shells (Arabian Cowrie) Gastropod; Family: Cypraeidae

There are over 200 species of cowries, which have slit-shaped openings lined with ridgelike teeth. The shells are ½ to 7½ inches long and very smooth, with a glossy, porcelainlike texture and vivid patterning and coloration. They were appealing to ancient civilizations who used them as ornaments, money, and religious symbols. Cowries are abundant in the tropical waters of the Pacific and Indian Oceans. Active at night, but hidden by day, these animals feed on algae around coral reefs.

Frog Shells (Spiny Frog Shell) Gastropod; Family: Bursidae

There are 60 species of frog shells, which have sturdy, thick, coarsely sculptured walls and are ½ to 10 inches long. They live in the warm shallow waters of the Caribbean and Red Seas, the Arabian Gulf, and the Pacific Ocean among coral and rubble. Frog shells are carnivorous, some feeding on marine worms. The larger shells were once used as oil lamps.

Moon Snails (Shark's Eye, also known as Atlantic Moon Snail) Gastropod; Family: Naticidae

Moon snails are a large family of smooth, glossy shells, $\frac{5}{8}$ to 4 inches long. They are found on sandy flats in nearly all parts of the world. Moon snails are carnivorous, feeding on other mollusks and similar creatures. They drill a neat hole through the shell of their prey and scrape out the meat.

Murexes (Spiny Murex) Gastropod; Family: Muricidae

Murexes are a vast family of at least 1,000 widely distributed species. They have attractive frills and long spines, and are 1 to 12 inches long. They live in various habitats, most being found in tropical seas on rocky shores, coral reefs, or stony, muddy, or sandy areas. Murexes are all carnivorous; some are able to drill holes in other mollusks, while others are able to wedge bivalves open by using a large projecting tooth on their outer lip.

Olives (Inflated Olive) Gastropod; Family: Olividae

There are over 300 species of olives, which have smooth and glossy shells $\frac{3}{4}$ to 5 inches long. They are highly colored or patterned. Olives are generally found in shallow water in warm tropical seas and are common in sandy areas. Most species lie hidden under sand during the day; they become active and feed on smaller mollusks at night.

Scallops (Remarkable Scallop) Bivalve; Family: Pectinidae

There are several hundred species of scallops, all of which have solid, almost circular shells 1 to 8 inches long, with low, rounded ribs. Scallops inhabit waters worldwide both temperate and tropical, feeding on plankton and other microorganisms. By snapping their shells together, scallops swim rapidly in a zigzag direction, usually to escape their major predator, starfish.

Screw Shells (Turret Nivea) Gastropod; Family: Turritellidae

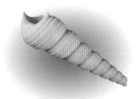

There are over 100 species of screw shells, which are long and pointed and have a dull finish and whorls that are rounded. These herbivores are 2¼ to 6½ inches long and live in shallow water on sand and mud in all the oceans of the world.

Tibia (Arabian Tibia) Gastropod; Family: Strombidae

Tibias are a very large group of long and slender shells 1 to 9 inches long. These vegetarians can be found in the deep warm waters of the Indian Ocean, the Philippines, and from Japan to Australia.

True Limpets (Long-Ribbed Limpet) Gastropod; Family: Patellidae

There are 400 species of limpets, which are round or oval-shaped, ¾ to 12 inches long. Limpets have a worldwide distribution, inhabiting rocky coastlines of all temperate seas. All are vegetarians.

Turbans (Tapestry Turban) Gastropod; Family: Turbinidae

There are about 500 species of these warm-water mollusks. Their shells are 1 to 8 inches long, often dark brown in color with mother-of-pearl interiors. Most species are vegetarian. Turbans can be found offshore in shallow bays or on reefs in the tropical waters of the South Pacific, Japan, the Philippines, Florida, the Caribbean, and New Zealand. Buttons are sometimes made from the shells.

Tusks (Octagonal Tusk) Scaphopod; Family: Dentaliidae

There are at least 1,000 known species of tusk shells. These mollusks have hollow tubelike shells that look like little elephants' tusks and are 1 to 4 inches long. Tusk shells are found worldwide in both temperate and tropical seas. These odd mollusks are without gills, head, eyes, or true tentacles. They are a carnivorous group, feeding on protozoans, foraminifera, and other microorganisms.

Venus Clams (Calico Clam) Bivalve; Family: Veneridae

There are over 400 species of venus clams living in both shallow and deep waters around the world. They have smooth shells, 1 to 5½ inches long, almost oval in shape. They feed on plankton and other microorganisms. Native Americans used to make wampum out of quahogs, a venus clam found along the eastern coast of the United States.

DATE DUE